Holy Words:
What Do They Mean?

Key Words Of Faith

David P. Rebeck

CSS Publishing Company, Inc., Lima, Ohio

HOLY WORDS: WHAT DO THEY MEAN?

Copyright © 1997 by
CSS Publishing Company, Inc.
Lima, Ohio

All rights reserved. No part of this publication may be reproduced in any manner whatsoever without the prior permission of the publisher, except in the case of brief quotations embodied in critical articles and reviews. Inquiries should be addressed to: Permissions, CSS Publishing Company, Inc., P.O. Box 4503, Lima, Ohio 45802-4503.

Scripture quotations are from the *Revised Standard Version of the Bible*, copyrighted 1946, 1952 ©, 1971, 1973, by the Division of Christian Education of the National Council of the Churches of Christ in the USA. Used by permission.

Library of Congress Cataloging-in-Publication Data

Rebeck, David P.
  Holy words : what do they mean? : key words of faith / David P. Rebeck.
    p. cm.
  ISBN 0-7880-1186-3 (pbk.)
  1. Christianity—Dictionaries. I. Title.
BR95.R36   1998
230'.01'4—dc21   97-29585
                                                                                                 CIP

This book is available in the following formats, listed by ISBN:
  0-7880-1186-3 Book
  0-7880-1187-1 IBM 3 1/2
  0-7880-1188-X MAC
  0-7880-1189-8 Sermon Prep

PRINTED IN U.S.A.

*This book is dedicated
to my wife Jeanette,
and our children, John and Ann,
through whom I learn to define
the love of God.*

Introduction

The farmer in the dell,
The farmer in the dell,
Hi, ho, the derry-o,
The farmer in the dell.

This opening verse of the nursery rhyme is well known, isn't it? The other verses and history may not be familiar, but at least this opening stanza is understood.

Or is it? What is your mental picture of this farmer? Where is s/he? In a dell, of course. Now then, what is a "dell"?

The meaning and significance of the Christian Faith are likewise diminished when key words are not understood.

Christians have a special vocabulary of holy words, but often have difficulty explaining what those words mean. As a result, blessings of understanding and spiritual comfort are less than full. This book is designed to help Christians express and appreciate the most important of faith's Holy Words.

Why does this need exist? Words of faith have weakened in meaning and significance for five reasons.

I. Words from ancient times have different meanings today.

For example, **justification** today means having an understandable excuse — however, in Biblical and Reformation times it meant nearly the opposite, that is, a deserved penalty accomplished. Another word with different meanings today is **evangelical**, which suggests conservative beliefs. However, it actually means gospel-centered. A third example is **catholic**, which today brings to mind the Roman Catholic Church — it originally meant "universal." Over time, words have developed meanings very different from their ancient origins, and their richness is either limited or misleading.

II. Some words are very difficult to define.

Holy is unquestionably a most important word of faith, used more than 650 times in the Bible. It is also used frequently in Church teaching, such as Holy Church, Holy Bible, Holy Communion, Holy Ones and Holy Spirit. Yet, what does **holy** mean? The same question could be asked of **glory, love** and **sin**. These are foundational words that should be understood; however, they have few well-known, easy to memorize and use definitions.

III. Some Biblical words have wonderful depth of meaning, but are used today without explanation.

Agape, koinonia and **Eucharist** are examples of Biblical words used today coming directly from their original languages. But what do they mean and why use them? There is absolutely nothing wrong with using ancient Biblical words today, but they need to be understood.

IV. On the other hand, rich lessons are lost because original languages are NOT used today. Important words from the Bible's original language may rhyme to teach a lesson, but that lesson is usually lost in English translations.

Both the Old and New Testaments use word plays to teach, even puns to make a point. For example, the Hebrew word for Adam is
  adam, who was created from
  adama, which is Hebrew for GROUND OR EARTH (Genesis 2:7).
The words are nearly identical in the ancient language to teach a lesson, but are very different in English.

V. The Bible often uses numbers as symbols, in contrast to the literal needs of today's scientific and technological society. But in

much of recorded history and true also in the Bible, numbers conveyed meaning beyond their count. For these reasons, the multitude of **144,000** in Revelation means more than a fixed number, but rather an immense and Godly complete multitude.

✟ ✟ ✟ ✟ ✟ ✟

After seventeen years as a parish Pastor, I see a great need for the meaning of Christian Holy Words to be grasped, appreciated, remembered, and shared. The goal of this book is to focus on approximately 130 frequently used Christian words providing short, easy to memorize and explain definitions. While this book is written in the Lutheran tradition, these topics are so much a foundation of faith that all Christians will find value in study and faith.

It is my prayer this resource will be of help both educationally and devotionally. For after all, words are but a means of the Good News — it is God's revelation in Christ Jesus that makes for Holy Words.

Rev. David P. Rebeck
Pentecost 1996

A Dictionary Of Holy Words

1 = unity

In the garden of Gethsemane, Jesus prayed the Father's goal, "that they may be **one**" (John 17:11, 22). As a result, Paul repeatedly stressed the unity of God's people ("there is neither Jew nor Greek ... but all are **one**" — Galatians 3:28).

This unity fulfilled in Christ Jesus had been also expected in the Old Testament. The foundational creed of the Hebrews was the *Shema* of Deuteronomy 6:4, "for the Lord your God is **one**." In another context, the basic understanding of mating is that, leaving father and mother, the two might become **one** (Genesis 2:24).

Unity is God's will in contrast to human tendencies to separate. To have other gods. To break apart in relationships. To be in dis-unity. Since the fall into sin, there have been divisions between man and God, husband and wife (Adam and Eve), children and descendents (Cain and Abel), and within society (tower of Babel).

However, as God brought order out of the chaos and darkness of the pre-created world (Genesis 1), so God wishes to bring order and unity into sin-distorted lives (Ephesians 1:9-12). This he ultimately did in Jesus Christ. Jesus became as we are, so that we might become as he is — in perfect unity with God and others. His tools are forgiveness and justification. His gift is received and shared by faith in "one Lord, one faith, and one baptism" (Ephesians 4:5). Consequently we ARE one, and the task of Christian ethics is to live up to that divine provision (Ephesians 4:15-16ff).

Being "one in Christ," therefore, has two aspects to it —

one accomplished,	one unfolding so that:
Christian unity is a	Christian living is a
Declared fact	Constant goal
God's doing	Human response

| Received by faith | An ongoing process |
| (Justification) | (Sanctification) |

"As therefore you **received** Christ Jesus the Lord, so **live** in him" (Colossians 2:6).

3 = of God

In a sin-broken world needing a unifying foundation, God is revealed in underlying orders of threes. Just as a "tripod" ("THREE FOOTED") has built-in stability, so the enduring presence of God shows itself in comprehensive threes:

- beginning, middle, end — (time)
- height, width, depth — (space)
- heaven, earth, under the earth — (creation)
- father, mother, child — (family)
- Father, Son, Holy Spirit — (God)

4 = Creation

Four is a symbol for Creation, the number being based on the four cardinal directions of north, south, east, and west or on the four ancient natural elements of air, earth, fire, and water. Four is used in the Bible to describe the created realm, such as the four rivers marking the boundaries of paradise (Genesis 2:10) or of earth and winds (Revelation 7:1). Where three symbolizes God, four symbolizes God's creation, the arena in which man lives and strives.

7 = God's presence IN the world; complete

Seven represents the completeness or harmony
of **God** (3)
IN (+)
His **created world** (4)

Seven conveys completeness, perfection and consummation between God and creation. It conveys harmony in and with nature. God is in his world and all is well. Therefore, seven is used to describe ways God fulfills his creation: resting on the seventh day (Genesis 2:2, 3) and commanding imitation (Exodus 20:10); observing seven Old Testament festivals (some lasting seven days, some in the seventh month); erasing economic debts every seven years (Deuteronomy 15:1-3); praying seven petitions in the Lord's Prayer and describing the heavenly realm in Revelation (seven churches, angels, lamps, etc. 1:20; 2:1). When seven is used, imagine how God is completing and fulfilling his created works.

10 = power

Ten gets its meaning and origin from the ten fingers we possess, handy in accounting! Ten increases whatever is there. It is also a way of describing very large numbers. Ten squared (100) and ten cubed (1000) are key multiples used to make whatever is referenced more powerful or significant.

12 = God's presence ON his creation; God's chosen

The number 12 is related to 3 and 4, as was seven; here they are <u>multiplied</u> together.

12 represents the impact **of God (3)**
acting **ON (x)**
His **created world (4)**

This helps interpret the meaning of
 twelve children of Abraham (Old Testament) and
 twelve disciples of Jesus (New Testament) as means by which God affected his world.

40 = testing in the world

40 is the result of **4 (creation)**
                      (x) multiplied by
                      10 (power)

This is a length of testing **in** God's created world. The Israelites were tested 40 years in the exodus (Deuteronomy 8:2; Numbers 32:13); correspondingly, Jesus was tempted 40 days in the wilderness (Matthew 4; Luke 4); the disciples were given 40 days after Easter to believe Jesus had risen (Acts 1:3); and the Church selected 40 days as a time before Resurrection Sunday during which the faithful might be tested during Lent.

144,000 = a huge multitude of faithful

A puzzling Biblical number is **144,000** in Revelation 14:1, 3. Some teach that it is a literal number of spiritual elite. However, building on the meaning of its parts, this number reduces to the following Biblical and symbolic factors: the

      12 tribes (of Israel)   (Old Covenant)   times (x) the
      12 disciples (and followers) (New Covenant) times (x)
    1000 (a huge multitude)   (10 x 10 x 10)   equals (=)
 144,000 = **a huge multitude of faithful** from all salvation history — much more than a fixed 144,000.

70 x 7 = infinite

Jesus said a repentant brother is to be forgiven **70 x 7** (Matthew 18:22). Is that limited to 490 times? No! Christians should forgive not only

    "completely," as God does in his world (7)
    not only a greater number of times than God (7 x 10 = 70) but
    both **multiplied** together (7 x 70)!

In other words, an **infinite** number — a greater number than God! This numerical expression is verbalized in the Lord's Prayer: "forgive us our trespasses as we forgive those who trespass against us" (Luke 11:4). There is no limit on either side.

Abba = dad

"Dad" is an informal translation of the Aramaic word *Abba*, but it captures some of the intimacy. *Abba* is used three times in the Bible, and each time is followed by the more proper name for father (*pater*). When used, it is in the sense of a desperate and intensely personal plea — Jesus in the Garden of Gethsemane, asking if the cup might be spared (Mark 14:36). The other two times are from Saint Paul (Romans 8:15 and Galatians 4:6), which refer to the Spirit pleading or crying from within. *Abba* is a word suggesting endearment and desperately appealing to a loving, close father.

Abraham = father of many nations God changed Abram's name to Abraham to underscore the promise of a multitude of descendants (Genesis 17:4-5).

Abram = exalted father (Genesis 11:26—17:4) See Abraham.

Adam = Adam, ground

Adam in English is pronounced the same as in Old Testament Hebrew — ADAM. It was used then, as now, as the proper name of the first man. But Adam is similar to another word that tells us something about ourselves. The connection is in Old Testament Hebrew where

> *adam* = ADAM and
> *adama* = GROUND, EARTH

By means of this rhyme, the very name of the first human was a reminder that having come from the ground (Genesis 2:7) life exists only because the "breath (spirit) of God" sustains it (Genesis 6:7). The Old Testament often teaches by using names to recall meanings. The meaning of **Eve** is explained in Genesis 3:20 **(mother of all living)**.

An additional relationship is taught by

> **man**, which is *ish* in the Hebrew, and
> **wo-man**, which is *ishah* (Genesis 2:21-24).

In this lesson of interrelatedness, the connection between man and woman is retained in English just as it is in the second creation account.[1]

Advent = coming

From Latin, Advent means "coming" and names the first season of the Church Year. Advent begins four Sundays prior to, and as preparation for, Christmas, reviewing the various ways Jesus comes as:

- prophesied
- announced by angels
- the Bethlehem babe of the virgin Mary
- John the Baptist's preparation
- returning Lord at the end of time

Agape = unconditional love See Love.

Alleluia = praise the LORD See Halleluia.

Alleluia is an English way of pronouncing the original and Hebrew *H*alleluia.

Alpha = beginning (and omega = end)

Three times in the Bible (Revelation 1:8; 21:6; 22:13), Jesus speaks of himself as the "Alpha and Omega." These are the first and last letters of the Greek alphabet, and mean "complete," just as we might refer to covering from "A" to "Z." The Greek letters *alpha* and *omega* are often used in Christian art and look like this:
αω or AΩ

Amen = so be it

Amen sounds and means the same in both the Old and New Testament Hebrew and Greek. Along with "halleluia," it is one of the most universal Christian words across languages and traditions of all periods. Often used in worship, it is also used throughout the New Testament epistles and indicates an enthusiastic (in-*theos* = in God) affirmation of God's doing. Contemporary worship may replace Amen with "Yes!" or "So be it!" A recently revived and very fine practice is to convincingly respond "amen" when receiving the Body and Blood of Jesus in Holy Communion.

Angel = a messenger

The New Testament Greek *aggelos* is pronounced very much like its translation **angel** in English. It is used 188 times in the New Testament, translated "angel" 181 times and "messenger" 7. It is a **bearer of an announcement** from God, a **messenger.**

Angels are especially important in framing the life of Jesus, as Gabriel foretold the birth of John the Baptist (Luke 1:13ff) and the conception of Mary (Luke 1:26ff). Angels also heralded Jesus' Bethlehem birth to the shepherds (Luke 2:15); comforted Jesus after his temptation (Matthew 4:11); announced the resurrection at the empty tomb (Luke 24:23, 24); and (although described differently), assured the disciples Jesus would return just as they had seen him ascend (Acts 1:10, 11).

Once "angel" even referred to a human. Saint Paul wrote, "I preached the gospel to you ... (and) you received me as an angel of God, as Christ Jesus" (Galatians 4:13, 14). In this respect, all Christians may be described as **angels = messengers of the gospel.**

Apostle = one sent See Disciple.

Apple = evil

"Apple" is a word used in every Sunday School. It is the kind of fruit from the tree of the knowledge of good and evil used to tempt Adam and Eve. However, Genesis 3:2, 3 doesn't actually describe the kind of fruit! Where did the idea of an apple come from?

The popular use of an apple comes from teaching the faith in Latin. In a way reminiscent of Hebrew wordplays and rhymes to teach a lesson, two Latin words were selected, where

malum = "apple" and
malis = "evil"

By this rhyme, the point was made to remind the student of faith that it is evil to give in to temptation, no matter how innocent it may appear. "Apple" in Latin was a memory aid that disobeying God is evil.

Ascension = going to heaven

This is a Latin word *(ascensio)* used to describe Jesus going (up) into God's heavenly realm (John 20:17).

Atonement = reconciled; At One (with God)

The meaning of atonement comes from the Old Testament and expresses God's canceling or pardoning of sin as a result of penitence and sacrifice. It comes from a Hebrew word meaning "to cover" (see Naked, for additional ideas). Particular emphasis was placed on an annual and still observed **Yom Kippur = Day of Atonement** in which that year's sins were held before God for pardon (Leviticus 23:27; Numbers 29:7-11). Atonement is rarely used in translating the New Testament, drawing a distinction between the Old Testament, where atonement was what **people** sought, with the once-for-all salvation of the New Testament, where atonement is what **Jesus** did. Rather, "reconciliation" is the word of choice to describe the result of our Lord's ultimate sacrifice (see 2 Corinthians 5:17-19, where reconciliation is the New Testament equivalent to atonement).

A non-Biblical but useful definition of **atone**ment is to separate the word into the parts **at-one**, for these two words put the gift of the gospel into clear and simple terms, that with sins forgiven, Christians are made "at-one" with God and one another.

Baptism = washing

Baptism is both a **name** (as a sacrament = holy act) and a **description** (washing).

The Greek word *baptismo* actually means "washing." What makes this word significant is what follows, that is, the Christian is baptized, or washed, "in Christ" or "In the Name of the Father ..."

Baptism = washing also continued Old Testament imagery of sins being washed away by the grace of God (Psalm 51). It provided the clear reminder that as water **washes away dirt,** so water with God's word **washes away sin** (1 Peter 3:21).

Benediction = good saying

"Benediction" is a Latin word used in a worship liturgy to convey a blessing from God. It is a *bene-* (GOOD) *diction (*SAYING), ordinarily taking the form God commanded Aaron (Numbers 6:23-27).

Bible = The Book (set apart for God's use) See Holy Bible.

Catechism = instruction; questions and answers on Christian teaching

The Greek word "catechism" means "to instruct by word of mouth." While not used in the Bible, the word "catechism" became popular with Martin Luther's written instruction in the **question** ("What does this mean?") and then memorable **answer** format (Small Catechism).

(Incidentally, Luther intended the Small Catechism to be used "by the head of the Household." Modern Christians would do well to honor that intent by teaching in partnership with the Pastor, to whom instruction is often exclusively entrusted. Mature Christians should also read Luther's Large Catechism, originally written for priests, but of such basic and clear content that it is useful for anyone in the modern literate world.)

Charismatic = grace-powered

In recent decades, charismatic has been used to refer to extraordinary **spiritual gifts** experienced by Christians and claimed to be similar to the experiences in Acts [healing, speaking in tongues (a foreign prayer language), and prophecy, for example (1 Corinthians 12-14)]. These witnesses may very well have something genuine to teach modern Christianity in the exercise of Biblical spiritual gifts.

However, charismatic is a **description** that Biblically refers to *every* believer!

Just as many cars are not "stick-shift" but auto-matic (SELF-POWERED), so all Christians are **charis-matic** (GRACE-POWERED).

Charis is the Greek word for God's **grace = undeserved love.** *All* believers are blessed with this Spirit-inspired (IN-SPIRITED) quality, and, while all may not experience the extraordinary gifts (such as those listed in 1 Corinthians 12), everyone is nevertheless "charismatic" by God in Christ Jesus and all are recipients of his Spirit. Saint Paul affirmed this in the very context of the extraordinary gifts by writing, "No one can say Jesus is Lord, except by the Holy Spirit" (1 Corinthians 12:3).

Christ = anointed one See Messiah.

Greek for Messiah.

Christian = follower of Jesus; living in Jesus

The word "Christian" is used only three times in the Bible (Acts 11:26; 26:28 and 1 Peter 4:16). As in the first reference, "Christian" originally was a flippant name given by the non-believing world to refer to **followers of Jesus.** However, as time went on, Christian was an identity to willingly claim, even die for (as in the Peter reference). By 100 A.D., "Christian" was commonly and proudly used by the faithful.

(Before it became popular, the favorite word in the New Testament for "Christians" was "brethren" or to a lesser degree "saints.")

Another aspect of the word "Christian" is similar to the way people today are named as belonging to and living in their city. In other words, those who live in Boston are Bostonians. So believers who live in Christ are Christians and **live in Him** (Colossians 2:6).

Church = assembly of believers See Holy Church.

Church Year

The Church Year is a division of the calender year into two halves and is used to organize Christian worship, **lectionary = (lessons)** and devotion. The first half outlines the life of Jesus beginning with the "season" of Advent, which starts a half-year "cycle."

The other half of the Church Year, the Sundays of Pentecost, focuses on Christian living and response to the life of Jesus.

The Seasons of the Church Year are:

Advent = the coming of Jesus
Christmas = birth of Jesus
Epiphany = revealing of Jesus
Lent = lengthening days approaching the light of
Easter = the resurrection, return of Spring and rebirth
Ascension = up to heaven (40th day after Easter — always a Thursday)
Pentecost = outpouring of the Spirit and its yield.

Concord = harmony

"Concord" is a Latin word meaning harmony and expresses the goal of the Christian movement and the Priestly Prayer of Jesus "that they may be one" (John 17:11). The word gained popular use from the Reformation era during which a collection of writings was assembled to unite the Lutheran movement. Called the *Book of Concord*, it contains the Augsburg Confession, both Small and Large Catechisms, other writings, and continues to unite and guide Lutheran Christians in doctrine and life.

Creed = I believe

"Creed" is from a Latin word, *credo* (literally, "I BELIEVE"). It refers to a statement or profession of belief and is also used to identify the three ancient and ecumenical statements of faith: the "Apostles'," the "Nicene," and the "Athanasian" creeds.

Devil = deceiver

"Devil" is the word of choice for the evil one in the New Testament, coming from the Greek *diabolos,* which means "deceiver."

While the Old Testament is framed in the context of a legal contract or covenant, the New Testament is based on grace and faith. So instead of the evil one being cast as a courtroom prosecutor as in the Old Testament (satan = accuser), the evil one in the New Testament is shown to be one who **deceives** the believer into doubt, despair, and faithlessness (1 Peter 5:8).

Disciple = student
Apostle = one sent

Jesus continued the symbolism and continuity of the Old Testament by choosing twelve disciples, just as there had been twelve children or tribes of Israel (see 12).

Throughout the Gospels, those twelve of Jesus were called disciples. Yet, generally beginning with the book of Acts, those same twelve (except Judas, replaced by Matthias, Acts 1:26) are called apostles. Why?

The answer has to do with Christian calling in general as well as giving direction for every believer. Consider: what event distinguished naming the twelve as disciples and apostles? The event was Pentecost Day (Acts 2) — the day the disciples were empowered with the Holy Spirit to begin their evangelistic work — the day they were commissioned and sent to spread the word.

This shift from "student" to "one sent" is reflected in the Greek words behind "disciple" and "apostle." These words are:

> **disciple** (*mathetes*) = **A STUDENT**
> **apostle** (*apostolos*) = **ONE SENT**

The difference between the two is that of role. In the gospel, the twelve were **students** (disciples) at the feet of the ***Rabbi = teacher***, Jesus.

Their role was to learn. However, after the Holy Spirit's power was given to them, their role was to **evangelize** — not just to learn, but themselves to be teachers and advocates of God's grace in Jesus. In fact, the word for apostle *(apostolos)* had a similar meaning in ancient Greek. It referred to a naval envoy, a representative of the king, who would carry his word or will to foreign lands. So the twelve, after Pentecost, were *ambassadors* for Christ (2 Corinthians 5:20), sent to proclaim God's word and will abroad.

Which are Christians today — disciples or apostles? Christians are *both* — at the same time having the mandate of learning (Matthew 11:29) as well as accomplishing the Great Commission (Matthew 28:19). This dual role explains why both ongoing Christian education as well as witness are equally commitments to honor.

Easter = rebirth/spring; The Resurrection

The word "Easter" is not from the Bible, but it is very symbolic. It comes from *eastre,* related to the coming of spring. Christians borrowed the symbolism of nature's rebirth after a cold, long winter to celebrate the resurrection. In a spiritual way, coming to faith is the rebirth of a person's soul out of a cold and dreary life of sin (1 Peter 1:23-25). These ideas were further blended in the King James Version of Acts 12:4, where the word for Passover was translated as Easter.

The date of Easter, which varies from year to year, does draw on Biblical roots. Easter is celebrated on different Sundays each year because it is dated by

- the first Sunday
- after the full moon
- after the spring equinox.

This means that during the season of Lent, as cold winter days are **leng**thening because the Sun's light is increasing, there is a point when the direct rays of the sun cross over the Earth's equator from the Southern hemisphere to the North, called the *spring equinox.* The spiritual symbolism for the Church Year is that out of the cold apparent death of winter (and Christ in the tomb) comes the rebirth of spring, warmth, and new life.[2]

Dating Easter *after the full moon* came from the dating of Passover and its symbolism (see Passover).

Easter is on a *Sunday* because Jesus rose from the dead on a Sunday (Matthew 28:1, 2), and ever since Christians have gathered on "day of the Sun" to celebrate the resurrection. As on our calendar today, this day was also "the first day of the week" (Acts 20:7). Easter is a grand annual recollection of that glorious reality and is dated to remind believers of God's promises and salvation history using
- Spring as a visual aid,
- the moon as a reminder of Old Testament deliverance, and
- Sunday on which to celebrate the resurrection.

Ecumenical = worldwide

Ecumenical comes from a Greek word *(oikoumene)* meaning "worldwide" or "universal" and is expressed in two ways. One is in referring to the three **"ecumenical" creeds** (Apostles', Nicene, and Athanasian). Sharing these ancient statements of faith worldwide is a common bond of faith for believers as they recite the "ecumenical" creeds.

From this comes another use of **ecumenical — an attitude —** that Christians strive to overcome divisions and show unity as the one body of Christ. Those with such vision are called the "Ecumenical Movement."

Eden = pleasure; Nod = wandering

Eden and Nod are a set of Old Testament words that teach by their meaning. They are the first two geographical places mentioned in the Bible (Genesis 4:16). But more important than their actual **location** (which is unknown), they are descriptions of two **conditions**!

That is, Adam and Eve were placed in paradise (Genesis 2:15), the Garden of **Eden**, which means **"pleasure and delight."** So it is with those who are in harmony with God.

Nod, on the other hand, means **"wandering."** That was the situation Cain found himself after breaking harmony with God by jealously killing Abel (Genesis 4:16).

Eden and Nod are more than **places**. They are **conditions** of living in or contrary to God's will (Deuteronomy 30:19).

Epiphany = revealing

This is a season of the Church Year which follows Christmas, precedes Lent, and comes from a Greek word meaning "revealing" or "showing forth." It is a time **revealing** the identity of the Christ child. During Epiphany, worship lessons include introduction and identification of Jesus, such as the coming of the Magi[3] with honor and gifts; Jesus' baptism (Matthew 3:13); the wedding at Cana (John 2) — the first miracle in John's gospel; and the calling of the disciples (Matthew 10:1, 2). Epiphany Season concludes with the ultimate revealing of Jesus' divinity in the Transfiguration (Mark 9:2).

Epistle = letter

"Epistle" is a Greek word *(epistole)* meaning a writing or correspondence. There are 21 epistles or letters in the New Testament written by Paul, James, Peter, John, and Jude. The word "epistle" is also used in modern worship to refer to the second of three lessons, usually from a New Testament epistle, but occasionally from the Old Testament, Acts, or Revelation.

Eucharist = giving thanks

Along with Lord's Supper and Holy Communion, Eucharist is another name for believers communing with Jesus through bread and wine and word. *Eucharist* is a Greek word used to describe what Jesus **did** as he instituted Holy Communion, namely, he **"gave** thanks" (*eucharisteo* — 1 Corinthians 11:24, 25). As a way of remembrance, Christians today "give thanks" through the "Eucharist." This also explains why the liturgy of Holy Communion in the Lutheran Book of Worship is titled "The GREAT THANKSGIVING."

However, there is much more to Holy Communion or Eucharist than simply remembering. It is more than just thinking. Holy Communion is not just an event to remember, a **thing to be done**, but it is an **action to be experienced**.

In the Eucharist, Christians are coming together as the Body of Christ, and then scattering back into the world to represent him. Throughout, there should be a joyous mood of thanksgiving in God's saving grace.

Evangelism = sharing the gospel

The English word "evangelism" looks very different from gospel and angel, but it is amazingly similar. *Angel* and *gospel* are **nouns** — a person or thing. *Evangelism* is the same word as a **verb** — an action! Here is the comparison, showing that

persons	*aggelos* (	ANGELS OR ANNOUNCEMENT)
bring	*euaggelion* (	GOOD-ANNOUNCEMENT)
which is called	*euaggelizo*	(BRINGING GOOD-ANNOUNCEMENT)

There are different ways of translating "evangelism," such as: preach(ed, ing), proclaimed, told, bring, brought, came, received, announced (the good news). However, everytime *euaggelizo* is used in the New Testament Greek, it is a **VERB** — an action. It would serve the Gospel well if Christians remembered evangelism is a verb, not just a noun; an action to be done, not just a thing to be talked about, and be aware of the call to daily witness as God's "angels" or ambassadors.[4] In fact, the English language might well be expanded to create a new word to show this: namely, gospeling! That is:

the gospel, *(euaggelion)* is proclaimed by Christians who do **gospel*ING*.** *(euaggelizo)* = **sharing the Gospel**

Evil, or evil one

The Greek word in the Bible for evil *(poneros)* can mean two things: it can describe an ungodly **event** as well as a **person.**

That is why the word in the Lord's Prayer petition "and deliver us from **evil**" can be translated either as "evil" or "the evil one" (John 17:15, for example). While the source is somewhat differently expressed, the result is the same — Christians can expect to be challenged or deceived into **sin = missing the mark** — misled by evil and/or the evil one.

This dual meaning for evil is also somewhat behind the fact that there are two Lord's Prayer translations in the *Lutheran Book of Worship*. One reads "deliver us from *evil*," while the other is translated "save us in the *time of trial*."

Whether "evil" means an **event** of temptation or **the tempter**, the occasion may be in **daily** challenges (Ephesians 6:13), or the **final** challenge at the end of time (also Ephesians 6:13). Either, probably both, may be the intent of the Lord's Prayer.

Forgiveness = this wrong shall not stand between us

How should "forgive" be defined? A common phrase says Christians should "forgive and forget" (which is nowhere in Scripture). This popular definition suggests forgiveness is, or at least includes, *forgetting* a wrong. In fact, how often do we "forgive" someone by saying "think nothing of it"?

However, only God can, or should, completely forget. Only God is able to "remember your sin no more" (Isaiah 43:25). Rather, in a sin-infected world, we must learn from past experiences and remember the wrongs that have occurred, even if we forgive them in another sense.

There is an interesting slogan about remembering:
"Fool me once, shame on you;
fool me twice, shame on me."
Did Jesus forgive sinners? Of course he did.
Did Jesus forget sins? No (although God does for Jesus' sake).

Whether it was anger at the Pharisees, bewilderment at his doubting disciples, or hanging on the cross, Jesus both forgave and *remembered* sin. What then, does Christ-like forgiveness mean? A useful definition is: **Forgiveness = this wrong shall not stand between us.**

There is a wonderful freedom and reality with this definition. It acknowledges the distinction between loving and forgiving the sinner yet addressing and dealing with sin and its consequences. With this definition, a Christian doesn't have to go through the guilt of unsuccesfully trying to forget sin. Rather, a Christian experiences the joy of not being at odds because of it.

Genesis = beginning

"Genesis" (which is pronounced in a similar way in both Hebrew and English) means origin, creation or **"beginning."** It is both the *name* of the first book of the Bible, as well as a *description* of God's creation in/of Genesis.

Glory = astounding radiance; praise and honor

"Glory" is a frequently used Biblical word which is very difficult to define. Simple definitions include "dignity," "honor," "praise" and "worship." However, even these lack the richness of the Greek word *doxa*.

Doxa is used 170 times in the New Testament, a rather high number. It is usually translated "glory" or "praise." There are some unique meanings, such as the long hair of women being their "pride" (1 Corinthians 11:14, 15) or describing the "brightness" of the light afflicting Saint Paul on the road to Damascus (Acts 9:3 with 22:11).

The best definition of glory includes two distinct directions:
— one *from* God to his creation (**astounding radiance**)
— the other, creation's response *to* God (**praise and honor**)

The first direction is **from God to his creation**. In this respect, God's glory is like light, and "shines" over the Bethlehem stable (Luke 2:9); is revealed in the transfiguration (Luke 9:31); blinded Saint Paul (Acts 22:11); is an image of the saints in heaven (Colossians 3:4); gives the persecuted eternal anticipation (1 Peter 4:13; Romans 8:18); and illuminates the darkness of sin (John 1). Such are images of glory from God.

The other direction behind the word *doxa* is **creation's response** to God's holy infiltration (Psalm 115:1; Matthew 5:16). It is a response of thankfulness combined with awe. From this sense come the actions of honor, praise, and worship. The liturgy word "doxology"[5] contains this sense.

While glory *(doxa)* remains a difficult word to define, dividing its direction two ways, *from* God (**astounding radiance**) and *to* God (**praise and honor**), helps give it depth and meaning.

Gospel = good news/announcement

The word for "good" in Greek is *eu*. It is often added to other words to signify their meaning as good. In this way, the New Testament refers to

| **persons** who bring | *aggelos* | (ANGELS OR ANNOUNCEMENT) |
| | *euaggelion* | (GOOD-ANNOUNCEMENT) |

This word *eu-aggelion* (GOOD-ANNOUNCEMENT) is always translated "gospel" in the Bible. **Gospel is a good announcement**. From this original meaning the title of the New Testament by the American Bible Society appropriately reads *Good News (for Modern Man)*. The gospel is literally "good news" or "good announcement." It is the will of God expressed in Jesus Christ for salvation — the best news ever heard.

Grace = undeserved love

"Grace" comes from the Greek *charis* (see also **Charis**matic), meaning grace, and refers to the perfect love God has for his creation. It is love not deserved or merited. That God perfectly loves sinners for Jesus' sake is at the root of the meaning of grace and the gospel (John 3:16).

God's grace is both a fact and an action:
    a **noun** (a **description** of what God thinks) as well as
    a **verb** (an **action** which God does).

Halleluia = praise the Lord

"Halleluia" is one of the most universal Christian words, traversing time and languages alike. It literally means "praise the LORD" (the "ia" = yah at the end being an abbreviation of Yahweh, a form of God's name — see Yahweh). It is directly from Hebrew, and should properly begin with a "hah" sound as it is in the original.

Halloween = hallowed (holy) eve

Halloween has a history and meaning related to All Saints' Day of the Church Year. In the Middle Ages, October 31 marked the end of the Celtic year — their "new year's eve." On that day, and especially evening, white-robed Druid priests gathered around sun-oriented monuments, such as Stonehenge, to appease the spirits of that year's dead. It was believed that on this last day of the year, the spirits of the departed would roam about, playing tricks on those left behind. To appease these spirits, potions and food were left out — "treats" given to avoid their "tricks." As the Christian Church grew in Europe, it tried to Christianize this new year's eve pagan festival by celebrating eternal life for those who had died, and thus dated All Saints' Day on the first day of the new year, November 1. The Sunday following All Saints' Day is also observed as "All

Saints' Sunday" to give thanks for the victory over death Christ has won for his faithful.

Holy = set apart for God's use

"Holy" is a tremendously important Biblical word, yet it is among the most difficult to define. Used over 650 times in the Bible (compared to "Jesus," for example, used just over 900 times), "holy" occurs in both Old and New Testaments and in Church theology, such as Holy Spirit, Holy Communion, Holy Church, Holy Bible, Holy Ones, and Holy Ministry.

But what does "holy" mean? The English word is used in common speech to refer to many things, religious and profane. Furthermore, there seems little resource for definition — it is surprising that many Bible dictionaries do not include "holy." Even Luther, when teaching the Second Petition of the Lord's Prayer (Hallowed [or holy] be Thy Name) assumes much when he explains "We should keep God's name *holy* ..." That is like answering a question with a question![6]

The word "holy" in both testaments of the Bible can be translated in many ways, such as "consecrated," "dedicated," and "blameless." A definition common to all is:

> **Holy = set apart,** or
> **set apart for God's use**

Holy is something or someone "dedicated" or "set apart" by or for God. This meaning reflects the Old Testament emphasis that God's chosen are a people **set apart** (from the Hebrew word ***kadosh*** or in English, "**kosher**").

Whether the *object* is
- a book (Holy Bible),
- God's presence (Holy Spirit),
- bread and wine (Holy Communion),
- an assembly of believers (Holy Church),

- Holy ones (Saints), or
- profession (Ministry)

this one fundamental definition of being **"set apart for God's use"** applies to all.

Holy Bible = the (set apart for God's use) Book

"Bible" means "book" and is a unique English title. For example, the German title is *Der Heilige Schrift*, meaning THE HOLY WRITING.

The word "Bible" is never used in the Bible! Instead, the Greek word ***graphe*** is used, which means "writing" (in English we say GRAPHIC). Likewise, the Romans used *scriptura*, which means A WRITING in Latin and is translated **Scripture** in English (2 Timothy 3:16 "all scripture is inspired by God").

The word "**Bible**" actually comes from the Greek *biblia*, which means "the **book**." (The English "*biblio*graphy" starts with this word.)

When used with Holy, **the Bible = the (set apart for God's use) Book**. It is Holy writing. Holy Writ. The Bible is a collection of writings treasured by the Church under the influence of God's Holy Spirit, to be holy = [set apart for God's use] for testimony, admonition, and salvation.

Holy Church = assembly of believers (set apart for God's use)

What is the "Church"? The most common answer is "a place in which Christians gather." In everyday speech, we hear, "Let's go to Church," suggesting the church is a place, and there *is* historic background to support this meaning. *Church* comes through the Old English *cirice* and German ***kirche***, from the Greek *kuriakon*, which means "**the Lord's house**" (where Lord = *kuria*).[7]

The word "church," however, is used to translate a Greek word very different in meaning. That word is *ekklesia* and it is *this* basic word that gives Biblical definition to the church.

Ekklesia (church) is a combination of two words:

ek - klesia
(OUT) (CALLED)

The church is people "called" "out" of the world into the Kingdom of God (1 Corinthians 1:2).

Ekklesia had a similar meaning in the everyday language of the ancient world. It referred to an assembly called out by a magistrate — a selection for a governmental position of responsibility. This word was adopted in the Bible to mean that God, the supreme of all rulers, is calling his people to responsibility in his kingdom.

Church as *ekklesia* is not just a **place** as in everyday conversation! The church is a select group of **people**, called by Jesus to be his followers. So 1 Corinthians 11:18 translates: "when you assemble *as a church*."

Ekklesia is also translated with words other than "church," such as "congregation" (Acts 7:38) and "assembly," (Hebrews 12:23), and is the root of the English word *ecclesiastical* = **of the church**.

It is noteworthy that the New Testament does not place adjectives before Church as we usually do today: That is, we might refer to the Lutheran Church, St. James Church, or Bible Fellowship Church. Instead, *Church* stands without introduction in the Bible. If anything, *Church* in the Bible is defined **after** it is mentioned, such as the Church *at Antioch* (Romans 16:1), or the Church *in your house* (1 Corinthians 16:19), and as a personification "greet(ed) the church" (Acts 18:22).

The church is an assembly of believers. It is relationship, not just a place. It is of God's doing, not limited to any particular congregation or denomination. In addition, it would be clearer if Christians emphasized not only the place but also the work of the church. That is, replace "let's go to church" with "let's go to *the* church *for* worship."

When used with Holy, the Church is an **assembly of believers** (called out set apart for God's use). This broad vision of believers called apart by and for God is the essence behind the four adjectives of the Nicene Creed — that the Church is "one, holy, catholic,[8] and apostolic."

Holy Communion = bread and wine (set apart for God's use)

Communion[9] comes from two Latin words:

> com - union
> (WITH) (UNITY)

Communion is a unity God wishes his people to experience. Whatever Christians do, they are to be mindful they represent "one Lord, one faith, one baptism" (Ephesians 4:5). Reflecting this unity, God's people gather around Jesus "in, with and under" the bread and wine of Holy Communion as the kingdom's oneness is shown and received. God's faithful experience that they are [set apart for God's use] by sharing [bread and wine]. This promise experienced makes Holy Communion one of the two **Sacraments** = Holy Acts.

Holy Spirit = God's power [set apart for God's use]; breath

An interesting place to begin understanding the Holy Spirit is with the English word "pneumatic." Street construction workers use a loud, chiseling "air hammer" to break up the road surface, also called a *pneumatic* hammer. This word is from the Greek language, translated:

> *pneu(ma) - matic*
> (AIR)   (POWERED)

That hammer is powerful, a tool of the worker, and powered by air *(pneuma)*. *Pneuma* (AIR, WIND, BREATH) *is the Greek word for Spirit* in the New Testament. God's Spirit is like the wind, a breath — it cannot be seen, but it is powerful and its effects can be felt.

Both the Greek *pneuma* and the similarly defined Old Testament Hebrew *ruach* use the visual aid of air/wind to name the Spirit.

The imagery of wind or air for the Spirit is richly used in especially the New Testament where the Spirit "blows" where it will (John 3:8) and "fills" believers (Acts 2:2-4). Many worship hymns also refer to the Holy Spirit being the "breath" of God, giving life to his will and empowering his people.

Along with this meaning as God's breath, there is another sense for the word *Spirit* — that of God's life creating and preserving power in general. When God breathed "the breath *(ruach)* of life" into Adam's nostrils, the same word translated "Spirit" is used.

The *Holy* Spirit, then, is **God's power** to accomplish his will as well as the creating and sustaining force that causes what it fills to be holy = **"set apart for God's use."**[10]

Hosanna = "save us, we beg you"

Hosanna is a Hebrew word acclaimed by the rejoicing and expectant crowds on Palm Sunday (Matthew 21:9).

Isaac = laughing one

More study should be done on the humor of God! What else would come from a loving God than the gentle tease of naming Isaac as the firstborn of Abraham and Sarah? The word *Isaac* means "laughing one!" *(yitschaq)*, named such because Abraham and Sarah "laughed" *(tsachaq)* when God predicted pregnancy very, very late in life (Genesis 17:17; 18:12). The fulfillment of that firstborn, nevertheless, proved God was trustworthy in his promises, a thought that certainly must have come to mind whenever Abraham or Sarah called for "laughing one!"

Israel = striving with God

Israel is a combination of two Hebrew words: *isra* meaning "striving" and *el* meaning "God."[11] It is characteristic of the Old Testament to teach by the very names of persons. In the case of Israel, the name of the Jewish nation was established when Jacob "strove" with God and prevailed (Genesis 32:28), just as all God's chosen are called to do (Luke 13:24). By remembering **Israel = striving with God**, Christians can claim a greater identity as God's nation and appreciate being the "New Israel" (Galatians 6:16).

Jerusalem = Zion; fortress; city of David See Zion.

Jesus = savior

The English name **Jesus** traces back through Latin (**Iesus**) to a Greek translation of the Hebrew *Joshua*, or more fully *Yehushuah*, which is rooted in "**YaHWeH** (or God) is salvation." YHWH is the Holy and unpronounceable name of God.

Just as many names have meaning in foreign languages (**David**, for example, is Hebrew for "**beloved**"), so the name **Jesus** has roots in the hope of God's saving presence and acts. The link with this name's history was especially important to the gospel writer Matthew. He explained the Bethlehem babe would be named "Jesus" "because he will *save his people* from their sins" (Matthew 1:21).

Because the name Jesus itself represented God's will, it was a common name for boys in the Old Testament era. It represented the hope of God's salvation to one day fully come. For this reason, the Bible makes clear *which* Jesus was the Savior by adding a description to his name, for example, Jesus the son of God (and others by relationship); Jesus of Nazareth (and others by place), and very frequently by role, Jesus (the) Christ.

Jesus as a given name ceased to be used shortly after the resurrection — the Hebrews discontinued using it to distance themselves from this acclaimed Messiah, while believers discontinued using "Jesus" as a given name out of respect for the Savior.

Justification = a deserved penalty accomplished

The word "justification" is an example of a word that has dramatically changed meaning over time. What does it mean today that "the act was 'justified' "? The connotation is that of legitimate excuse — that there was a "just" reason, even if the action was not. We don't really blame someone whose harmful actions are justified, especially in a society in which a person is innocent until proven guilty.

Now think about the classic profession of faith — "we are justified by faith" (Romans 5:1; 4:28). Modern usage suggests we are *excused* the guilt of sin and not to blame.

However, from Biblical times through the Reformation period the meaning of justification was not an **excuse**, but the *execution of a deserved penalty*. Getting your **just** desserts, we still say today. **Justified** meant **justice** being carried out. Jesus died. We ARE guilty. We have no excuse for sin, and our salvation is not because we have any "just" defense to merit God's sympathy. This understanding of justification as punishment for deserved wrong instead of acquittal deepens appreciation for the sacrifice of Christ, who became sin (an **"expiation"** = substitute — Romans 3:25) and died for believers. This meaning is very clearly and Biblically expressed in the hymn "Just As I Am, **without one plea.**" Jesus did not excuse, he redeemed by taking our deserved penalty of death upon himself.

Koinonia = fellowship

The Greek word *koinonia* is the word behind the Latin-based "communion" (WITH UNITY) and links to such words as *koinos* (SHARED BY ALL) and *kolonia* (COLONY).

It is similar to the way the English word "commune" (A SHARING SOCIETY) is related to "communion" (WITH UNITY).

The basic idea is that of "sharing," frequently translated as "fellowship" (Acts 2:42). When used in the New Testament, context determines what **kind** of sharing is being emphasized. There are four types of translation of New Testament *koinonia*:

- partnership   shared responsibility (Philippians 1:5)
- fellowship   shared relationships (1 Corinthians 1:9)
- contribution   shared resources (Romans 15:26)
- participation shared bread and wine (only one verse: 1 Corinthians 10:16)

In recent church-life, Koinonia is also used as a name for a Church fellowship or activity group, underscoring the many forms of unity Christians enjoy.

Kyrie = Lord

This is from a Greek word (*kurios*) that refers to someone in authority over another (Matthew 6:24). In faith, it can refer to God (Matthew 21:9), to Jesus (Matthew 8:8), and even once about the Spirit of Jesus (2 Corinthians 3:17).

In worship, Kyrie refers to prayer and the petition **"Lord, have mercy."** The full phrase sometimes sung or spoken is **"Kyrie eleison."** It usually follows a confession of sin early in the liturgy and asks that the consequences of sins, now assuredly forgiven, might be lessened.

Laity = people; clergy = organizer/overseer

"Laity" or "lay" persons come from a Greek word, *laos*, which means "PEOPLE." It refers to *all* believers who are "called" by the Gospel into faith (1 Peter 2:9). (See Church = *ekklesia* = called out.) As reflected in the companion word "clergy," the Bible also recognized some believers are "called," that is, "set apart" into the professional ministry and function as "clerics" or organizers of the Christian movement (Ephesians 4:11-13). It is important to notice that the difference between laity and clergy, however, is one of function, not value. *All* believers are "priests" (a very important lesson from Martin Luther) to carry forth the Great Commission (Matthew 28:19).

Lent = *leng*t*hening days

Lent is a period of days approaching the light of Easter, return of Spring, and nature's rebirth. Lent is a forty-day observance of the Church Year during which the faithful prepare to celebrate the sacrifice and resurrection of Christ. See also Easter and the number 40.

Liturgy = worship order

Liturgy is based on a Latin word meaning "work of the people." It came to refer to the participation of worshipers with preselected responses of song and text. Liturgy refers to the Order of Worship as it is used today, with roots going back over 1700 years.

Love = becoming like Jesus

Jesus and Peter had an interesting conversation about love in John, Chapter 21. Three times Jesus asked, "Simon, son of John, do you love me?" Three times Peter answered, "Lord; you know that I love you." In fact, the third time, Peter was "grieved" at Jesus' repeated inquiry. The problem was Jesus and Peter were speaking of love on different levels.

The confusion is that "love" in English covers a tremendously wide variety of feelings and relationships. The original Greek language of the New Testament was much more precise. There are four different Greek words translated as "love" in English. They are:

1. *agape* = a highly ideal and selfless affection or charity. This is God's perfect love (*agape* is used 258 times in the New Testament).

2. *eros* = a love uniquely, if not sexually, expressed between a male and female (and from which English derives "erotic"). This word is not used in the New Testament.

3. *phileo* = to be a friend or close like a brother (from which the U.S. city *Phila*delphia is named). *Phileo* is used 26 times in the New Testament, generally translated as "love" and occasionally as a "brotherly kiss" (as in the betrayal of Jesus, Luke 22:48).

4. *sturgus* = natural affection, rooted primarily in kinship and used only twice (Romans 1:31; 2 Timothy 3:3 and in a negative sense, i.e., "unnatural affection").

As the numbers show, *agape* and *phileo* are most frequent in the New Testament.

Agape is the love God shows to man — perfect, gracious, ideal, unconditional, without merit on our part (John 3:16; 1 Corinthians 13).

Phileo is the love people develop — sometimes close to *agape*, but more often in a mutually satisfying way of expected give and take.

What does this background mean? It illustrates that the Bible is very realistic about our ability to love humanly as we have been loved by God. While we strive to exhibit *agape*, often the best we can do is *phileo*.

These words represent both **fact *(agape)*** and **process *(phileo)***, reflecting the relationship between **justification** and **sanctification**. That is, by the undeserved love of God *(agape)* we are made completely righteous, just and holy. However, while totally redeemed in God's sight because of his perfect love *(agape)*, we strive, if not struggle, to live up to our declared value as righteous, which is the process of sanctification. Love in human and sin-infected lives is *phileo*, although we enjoy grace while striving toward the goal of God's perfect love *(agape)*.

This is essentially the lesson behind the exchange between Jesus and Peter referred to above. Jesus began by asking, "Simon ... **do you love *(agape)* me?**" Simon Peter replied, "Lord, you know **that I love *(phileo)* you.**"

The conversation points out the reality that while God loves perfectly, we can but strive to the best of human limitation or ability.

But we still have not arrived at a definition for what is commonly expressed as Christian "love." An unusual but useful definition is "**becoming like Jesus.**" This is obviously not a Biblical quotation, but it contains some key features.

First, for us to love as God loves us is a **process** toward which we strive (sanctification). It is the Christian's goal to become more like Jesus and therefore more influenced by God's perfect love. "What would Jesus do in my place?" is a good "process" question to raise. Whenever we ask this question in any time of uncertainty, God's Holy Spirit will help inform faith and life in ways that help in the ongoing process to become like Jesus.

How is this done, given the constant tug of sin? Consider Paul's frustration of being "between a rock and a hard place" — "I do not do the good I want ..." (Romans 7:19). Paul's unique and practical advice is to **imitate** (Hebrews 13:7; also see 1 Peter 2:21 and Philippians 4:9).

Third, Christian love, as a process and aided by imitation, is **not necessarily an emotion, but an action**. In other words, the unachievability of *agape* as an emotion doesn't mean we cannot *act* in love and therefore become more like Jesus. This sense of love as action, not necessarily emotion, is the reason "love" has been translated "charity" in Bible translation. Indeed! Where in the Bible is love described as an emotion to experience? Instead, love is expressed in action. God's action in Jesus. Disciples' actions in deed. Our actions in imitation of Jesus. It is wonderful if the heart joyfully participates in an endeavor, but God calls us to response, not sentiment. Many Christians experience guilt because they do not "love" as Jesus did. But this guilt can be eased by recognizing love can be God-pleasing as an action and not necessarily an emotion.[12]

Consider the life of Jesus himself. Did everything he **did** come from a motivation of love? Yes. But did Jesus **feel** love at all times? No.

Imagine Jesus in agony on the cross, forsaken by God (Matthew 27:46). Recall Jesus in anger driving the money changers out of the Temple (John 2:14-16) or Jesus calling the religious officials a **"brood of vipers"** (Matthew 3:7). (Today we would say **"snakes in the grass."**)

At such times Godly love was an action more than an emotion. So also with us, and more. Even when we cannot feel love, we can act in love with good conscience. As a result, two things happen. One is that often the emotion of *agape* grows. (Recall how you feel after you HAVE acted in love or prayed for an "enemy.") Moreover, by acting, or imitating Jesus, we grow in Godly love, and by striving to love, do, in fact, increasingly **become like Jesus**.

Messiah = anointed one

It was the practice in the Old Testament to honor new leaders by anointing them with oil (Exodus 28:41). In a dry and parched environment, fragrant and soothing oil would be a pleasant and skin-softening gift. The best would be used to set apart the most honored leaders. The Hebrews looked forward to the day when God would send the very best of leaders, whom they called the Messiah (Isaiah 61:1 — "anointed" from the Hebrew word *Mashiyach*). Through his anticipated leader, God would ultimately deliver his people, and to this leader God's people would devote the highest honor. Jesus was that hope fulfilled and proved to be the promised Messiah, anointed by God himself to accomplish deliverance from sin and death (Luke 4:18).

Naked = exposed!

It might seem odd to include **naked** in a dictionary of Holy Words, but Genesis uses one of the most unique word rhymes in Scripture here, and the spiritual symbolism is enlightening.

The lesson is from rhyming words and is regarding falling into sin and its consequences. That is, the serpent was the most

> **"subtle"** *(arum)* of creatures (Genesis 3:1) and was later **"cursed"** *(arar)* (Genesis 3:17).
> By disobeying God, Adam and Eve were then affected and noticed they were
> **"naked"** *(arur)* (Genesis 3:7, 10).

Since the Hebrew words in bold italics rhyme, it is likely the author wanted readers to make the connection that deception by **satan** resulted in **exposure** and **God's wrath**! This illustration is in Paul's mind when he urges readers to "put on Christ" (Galatians 3:27) to cover the exposure of sin (Revelation 16:15).

Nave = ship

The word "nave" describes the main seating area of a worship building. What is less known is the word comes from the Latin *navis* which means "ship" and from which comes the English word "navy." In Church architecture, gathering in the "nave" reminds believers that they, carried by Christ's Church (= assembly of believers), are saved from sin's drowning, just as a boat delivers its occupants. Sometimes Church buildings are intentionally shaped like an ark (bringing to mind Noah, or Jesus stilling the waters). In addition, those in pews might be thought of as rowers lined and pulling together, and the chancel (front area) like the captain's quarters in the stern. When sitting in worship, look around to imagine how your sanctuary might suggest the image of being carried in a boat through one life to the next.

Nod = wandering   See Eden.

Paraclete = helper; Holy Spirit

"Paraclete" comes from a New Testament Greek word *(parakletos = standing on one's side)* that may refer to Jesus as a helper, advocate, or comforter (as in 1 John 2:1, for example) but is generally used to refer to the Holy Spirit. Jesus promised his disciples he would send "another counselor or comforter" *(parakletos)* — John 14:16. Paraclete is little used today and most Bible translations avoid it. However, Paraclete is more frequently used in hymn texts to refer to the Holy Spirit.

Paschal See Passover.

Passover = pass-over

Passover is a supreme Jewish celebration each year. The week-long festivities recall how God delivered Israel by sending the angel of death as the tenth plague upon the Egyptians (Exodus 12:11ff). For those who heeded Moses and in faith sacrificed a male lamb, the angel of death "passed over" their homes, sparing the lives of Hebrew firstborns.

The lesson of obedient faith is again evident in the Lord's Supper when Jesus, celebrating the annual Passover meal with his disciples, was himself the New Testament "Lamb of God," so that the angel of death and destruction might forever "pass over" believers and Jesus become the firstborn to be saved from eternal death (Colossians 1:18). The Hebrew word behind "to pass over" *(pasah)* is the root behind the English **Paschal** — as in Paschal Candle — and refers to Jesus as the Passover Lamb.

Passover is dated in the spring and near Easter each year and likewise shifts dates from year to year. This is because the Hebrew calendar was, and still is, guided by the phases of the moon. Since the Passover event in Egypt took place during a full moon (giving the Israelites light by which to travel at night), that full moon marked what was and still is the first day and month of the Hebrew calendar.

Pentecost (season/day of) = harvest; 50th

There is much to understand about the event and meaning of Pentecost. On the surface, the word mirrors the Greek number "fifty." And, in the life of Jesus, Pentecost *was* the fiftieth day after the Resurrection. But besides the Acts 2 event bestowing the Spirit's power, Pentecost had already been one of the seven major Jewish festivals for hundreds of years (Exodus 34:22; Acts 2:1)! For the Hebrews, Pentecost was an annual festival celebrating the **first harvest** (of wheat and barley) which concluded 50 days later with the **second harvest** (of olives and grapes).

When Acts 2 describes the disciples gathered on the day of Pentecost, they were gathered in celebrating something like American Thanksgiving. It is a tremendous lesson that on the annual Old Testament festival celebrating the beginning of harvest, God chose to send the power of his Son's Spirit to empower growth in the New Testament kingdom.

Since Jesus' powerful spirit has now been granted, Pentecost is celebrated by Christians as a season. It is an era until Jesus comes at the end of the age to gather in and conclude the harvest of which he is seed and we are caretakers. The first harvest — the resurrection of Jesus — had been accomplished and the time is ready to begin preparations for the second harvest yet to come.

Peter = rock

Peter comes from the Greek word *petros*, which means "ROCK." Named such by Jesus (Matthew 16:18), Peter proved to be a solid, although very human, witness upon which to learn of Jesus and God's love.

The interpretation of Peter as "rock" is very differently viewed by Lutherans and Catholics in that Catholics view Peter, **the person** (and therefore first pope) to be the rock; Lutherans view Peter's **confession** (and all who likewise believe) to be the rock.

Prophecy and Prophesy

These words are included not so much for definition, but for accuracy in pronunciation, especially in public worship reading. They both are used in translating Old and New Testament predictions of future events. The difference is that *prophecy* (pra-fe-see) is the prediction itself, while *prophesy* (pra-fe-sigh) is the action of making the prediction.

Repent = think again (change, and do what is right)

"Repent" comes from Latin *re-* (TO DO AGAIN) and *pent,* a root for "PENANCE" and "PENITENCE." It means to feel sorry and turn from sin. The Greek New Testament word is similar: *meta-* (AGAIN) *noeo* (THINK). Jesus used this word not only to call sinners from sin (Luke 5:32), but also to call his disciples from misconceptions (Acts 11:18).

Sabbath = rest

When recalling the Second Commandment, "Remember the Sabbath day ..." many Christians equate **Sabbath** with Sunday. Not so. The Hebrew word *sabbat* means "rest." Just as God rested on the seventh day, so people should do also.[13]

The link between Sabbath and Sunday comes in part from Luther, who explained that Christians observe the Second Commandment by focusing on God's Word once a week, typically by means of worship on Sundays (Sunday being a weekly anniversary of the resurrection).

The meaning of Sabbath as rest, however, is more clear in the modern word "sabbatical," which is time off from work for recreation or refreshment.

Sacrament = holy (set apart for God's use) act

Any word that begins with *sacra* (which is Latin) or similarly, such as *sacred, sanctify, sanctuary,* and *sanctification,* comes from the meaning of holy, namely, "set apart for God's use." A Sacrament = a holy act. In the Lutheran tradition, there are two Sacraments, Baptism and Holy Communion, because by Lutheran definition a Sacrament must

- use a physical element (water, bread, wine);
- be commanded by Jesus;
- be a means of grace and forgiveness.

Saint = a person (set apart for God's use); holy one

"Saint" is very similar to the word "Holy" in the New Testament because

> holy in Greek is *agnos*
> saint in Greek is *agnon*
>
> Notice how similar the Greek words are, yet how different the English is!
> That is because while they are the same Greek root word, they are different "forms of speech."
> holy *(agnos)* is an adjective and
> saint *(agnon)* is a noun
> The distinction between these two words is that
> holy is a "set apart" *thing,*
> saint is a "set apart" *person.*

Many times Christians say, "I'm no saint," admitting they are not perfectly living out God's will. However, there is more to Christian identity than trying to be perfect — and that is God's declaration that Christians are holy for Jesus' sake. Sins have been cleansed "white as snow" (Isaiah 1:18). They are forgiven and forgotten by

God for the sake of faith in Jesus. To be a saint is *God's doing* in Christ Jesus. All Christians ARE saints!

While Christians do strive to live up to that identity (**sanctification** [*sanctus* = HOLY and root of *sanctify*]), we are nevertheless saints and declared holy for Jesus' sake (**justification**).

That declaration of being holy = set apart for God applies to both Christians who are living as well as those who have passed into eternity. You don't have to die to be a saint! The New Testament makes frequent appeal to "the saints" (Ephesians 4:12; Romans 1:6) — including believers *living* as well as those who have entered Paradise. Saints are all God's people redeemed by Jesus who are *now* (and forevermore) holy = set apart for God's use.

Salutation = greeting

Saint Paul often sent greetings or "salutations" in his letters. A saluation is a "salute" with words, a way of wishing others well (and reflecting the Hebrew *shalom* = well-being, peace). Modern Christians use the word *salutation* to name a greeting in worship, especially using the phrase "The Lord be with you." Although this phrase is rare in the Bible (only once in the New Testament [2 Thessalonians 3:16]; and using LORD [for God] in six Old Testament references), it is a very ancient and widely used greeting in liturgical worship. Often "The Lord be with you" is a way for the Pastor to say "hello" before worship. The correct response to this salutation by worshipers is "And also with you."

Sanctification = becoming holy = set apart for God's use

Sanctification is a lifelong process of becoming as Jesus is, holy = set apart for God. See Index for other references to compare sanctification with justification.

Satan = accuser

The Old Testament refers to the evil one as "satan." The Hebrew word is pronounced very much like the English and means "accuser." The image of Satan as an accuser of God makes sense because the Old Testament relationship between God and his people was in a form of a **legal agreement** (also called **covenant** or **testament**).

That is, God pledged to do some things (preservation, blessing, promised land) if his faithful did what was required (no other gods, witness, do justice, obey the commandments — Deuteronomy 4:37-40; 6:20-25; 7:11-13). God, in his heavenly "court," would give blessing or curse in proportion to his verdict. Just as in a courtroom today, there would be both defense counsel and prosecutor. In the Old Testament, the prophets, Scripture, and Spirit were on God's defense; the prosecutor or "accuser" was satan.

An illustration of satan as God's accuser is in Genesis. Assuming the same evil one is represented by the serpent and satan (Revelation 12:9), notice how Adam and Eve are led to doubt God by careful insinuation: "Did God say, 'You shall not eat of ANY tree in the garden?'" (Genesis 3:1). Satan accuses God's will and mistakes his words.[14] Satan works to overthrow God's will. In the book of Job, even God himself is put on trial!

In this context, the hope of the Old Testament faithful was to one day welcome God's ultimate advocate to overcome satan and thus establish an everlasting kingdom of justice and peace (Isaiah 9:6, 7).

When used in the New Testament, this definition of satan as accuser explains the meaning of Jesus' harsh-sounding words to Peter. When Peter renounced the foretold crucifixion, Jesus said to him, "Get behind me, satan." Jesus didn't mean that Peter was now the disdained evil one of God, but that Peter was in the inappropriate role of questioning or accusing the wisdom of God's will. Christians are well aware of the presence of doubt and questioning, and are no different from Peter. Not that we are disdained by God, but that the evil one is present affecting us, distorting God's truth and influencing choices.[15]

Shalom = well-being; peace

Shalom is a Hebrew word which is still used. The simple definition is "peace"; however, there is more to it. Shalom is not just absence of conflict, evil, or war, but the presence of well-being and satisfaction. This is the full and true peace Jesus fulfilled and of a kind "not as the world can give" (John 14:27).

Sin = separating from God; missing the mark

Sin is an opposite of *holy* where holy = set apart *for* God's use; sin = whatever separates *from* God.

Romans 3:23 is helpful: "... all have sinned *(hamartano)* and *fall short of the glory of God.*" Sins *(harmartia)* are anything which separates us from God. While God calls us to be holy = set apart for HIS use, there are internal and external temptations that lead us astray and cause us to fall wayward.

This is precisely a basic Greek definition of *harmartia*. The word in Biblical times was used in traveling and referred to choosing the wrong road! This became a good visual aid for this word as "sin" — that of choosing the wrong way or path when dedicated to walking with God (and didn't Jesus warn of the broad and narrow directions? — Matthew 7:13, 14). In short, sin (from *harmartia*) is going astray and therefore **separating from God**.

There is another useful image behind this word for "sin." *Harmartia* was also used in ancient times in athletics. It meant to "miss the target" or "miss the mark" and thus forfeit the prize. This visual aid is useful in expressing the Christian faith because it suggests both goal and consequence. That is, the goal of a follower of Jesus is to be "on target" in the imitation and life of our Lord, not to "fall short of the glory of God." The consequence of "missing the mark" is to bring dishonor and discomfort in failing, to say nothing of the potential of losing one's eternal prize and heavenly crown. Paul expressed this goal in athletic terms in 2 Timothy 4:7, 8.

Borrowing from sharpshooting, a modern illustration for sin in this sense is **failing to hit the bull's-eye**. Whether it is archery or another kind of target shooting, the goal is to hit the center of the target, not one of the outer concentric rings. Sin is anything less than the "bull's-eye of God's perfect will."

This definition of "missing the mark" fits the theology of sin very well. We cannot avoid sin. No matter how hard we try or practice, we still can be wildly off target. And even when it appears we have struck center, careful measurement shows that we have only come very, very close. Both the impossibility of perfection and the clear fact of what is expected are common to this visual aid and Biblical witness of the meaning of sin as **missing the mark**.

In these respects, forgiveness is an opposite of sin, in that as sin = missing the mark of God's will, separating from God; forgiveness = this wrong (or shortfall/shortcoming) shall not stand between us.

Spirit See Holy Spirit.

Sunday = day of the *Sun* (the day on which Jesus the *son* of God rose from the dead)

God caused the resurrection to occur on a Sunday. The Greek and Roman calendar had already honored the Sun by placing it as the first day of the week, as we still do today. They worshiped the Sun for its power to give light, warmth, and provision. Now Jesus, the "true light of the world" (John 8:12), had come, dispelling all other relative darkness! In addition, the Caesar, lord of the Roman empire, was believed to be a "reflection" of the sun with its power and was also honored as a god. What better day could God have chosen to teach of Jesus Christ as true God and ultimate Lord over all?

Theology = study of God

Theology is knowledge and witness of God and his will. The ending *"ology"* means the "speaking or profession of" and *theos* means GOD in Greek.

Translation = writing between languages

"Trans" means to go across. A translation is a writing that communicates a foreign language as accurately as possible in another language. The Bible was written long ago in ancient languages of Hebrew, Greek, and some Aramaic. English wasn't even in existence when any of the Bible was composed. Throughout time, languages changed and new "translations" had to be written so old books could be understood. In the Roman Empire, the Bible was translated from the original languages into Latin. Martin Luther in Germany translated Scripture into German. King James in England authorized an English translation in 1611. And translations continue to be written in different languages, even in different ways in English, so the original words can be most accurately understood.

Trinity = God is three in one

"Trinity" is another very familiar word not used in the Bible. It came into Christian usage through the writings of an ancient theologian named Tertullian. Around 200 A.D. he applied a Latin word based on three (*tri*, as in tri-pod or THREE-FOOTED) to refer to God as three in one (Father, Son, and Holy Spirit). His word *"trinity"* became quickly accepted.

Yahweh = saving God

What is God's name? The Bible uses "god" to refer also to other gods (as in the first commandment) just as English does.

Abraham wondered about this also and asked God, "Who shall I say has sent me?" God replied, "*I Am* has sent you" (Exodus 3:14). God didn't give so much a name as a description. Throughout the Old Testament, however, there IS a name for God — in the original Hebrew it is similar to the English consonants: YHWH.

But try to say YHWH! It cannot be done and this was God's intent. YHWH cannot be spoken and *therefore cannot be abused*! In ancient times, names were not only precious and with definition, but suggested power and mastery. (Things aren't so different today. For example, we think we have mastery over "electricity," but what exactly is it, really?) So with God, a spoken name wasn't granted because there is to be mystery and awe in speaking of God.

Mystery and awe are respectful, but not necessarily helpful when reading, teaching, or believing! So, while still safeguarding the unpronounceable name of God as YHWH, three speakable names have developed — Yahweh, LORD, and Jehovah.

I. Yahweh The origin of **Yahweh** used in some translations and much Christian literature comes from imagining vowels between the letters YHWH, resulting in a name that can be spoken. This is a popular English way of respectfully speaking God's name and is pronounced "yah-way."

II. LORD Another way to respect YHWH is to replace it with another word. This is exactly what was done in the Old Testament and in many English Bible translations. In place of YHWH, **LORD** is written and spoken (in all capital letters in English to show it replaces YHWH). This practice explains the apparent doubling of God's name. For example, in much of Genesis there is reference to "LORD God." In Hebrew this is "YHWH *Elohim*" where *Elohim* is a generic word like English "god." "LORD God" precisely named the deity being described but could not be spoken out loud. Whenever LORD in capital letters is used, it is a substitute for the Holy and unpronounceable proper name given for God, YHWH.

III. Jehovah The third name to evolve from YHWH is **Jehovah**. There is a historical accident here! That is, the Hebrews originated the idea of saying LORD instead of YHWH, as described above. To do this, in Hebrew Bibles the vowels of the Hebrew word for **Lord** = *(adonai)* were placed above YHWH. This reminded the Hebrews to say Lord instead of trying to say YHWH.

This fact became forgotten over the centuries, however, and when King James authorized the English translation of 1611 A.D., the sounds of YHWH and the vowels of Lord were put together to create *Jehovah*. Therefore, *Jehovah* is an invented word, not truly Biblical. (It is still used, however, in hymns. When sung, think of "LORD God" when Jehovah is used.)

Zion = Jerusalem; fortress; city of David

Over 160 times in Scripture, and in many hymns, *Zion* is used as another name for Jerusalem. Zion refers to "God's holy hill" (Psalm 2:6) or "mountain" (Joel 3:17), which is also Jerusalem (Psalm 51:18). Jerusalem, which is located on a hill or small plateau, was therefore easy to defend and thought of as a fortress. Also, being elevated (and therefore closer to God), Jerusalem/Zion was host to the Temple and represented the presence and protection of God (Psalm 135:21). The title "city of David" (2 Samuel 5:7) refers to the same place, since King David led military efforts to conquer the area for the Israelites with Jerusalem becoming capital. In the New Testament, Zion/Jerusalem is extended into the heavenly kingdom (Hebrews 12:22; Revelation 14:1), representing the perfected and eternal presence and protection in God's never-ending community.

---

1. By study of the language, style, and viewpoint, Bible scholars generally agree there are two creation accounts in Genesis. God inspired the author of Genesis to record both rather than combine them and therefore blur the insights each uniquely represents. The two accounts of creation are:
  Genesis 1:1—2:4a (where the transcendent God is called *Elohim* in a repetitive and systematic style with a universal concern and watery beginning—and the end of creation is: trees/animals, then man/woman) and
  Genesis 2:4b—3:1 (where an imminent God, *Yahweh Elohim,* is portrayed in a picturesque and personal style with an earthly concern and desert beginning — and the end of creation is man, trees/animals, then woman).

2. The image of Lent to Easter symbolized by winter to spring is a fine illustration. However, it "works" only in the Northern hemisphere! Just the opposite is happening in the Southern Hemisphere, where summer is turning into fall. Since it is estimated that around 2000 A.D. there will be more Christians in the southern half of the world than the North, it is this author's belief a constant date and symbolism for Easter will be developed by the next generation, just as a fixed date for Christmas is now observed.

3. **Magi**, referred to only by Matthew, Chapter 2, were actually **Persian astrologers**. In their age they were "wise men" in that they would study the heavens to note the changing of seasons, calibrate periods of time, and, similar to horoscopes today, look for predictive signs. God led them to acknowledge that a great thing had happened in Bethlehem, and they represented the **Gentile** (which means **non-Jew**) adoration of Christ in parallel to the Jewish shepherds. (A relationship to the supernatural is underscored by this word Magi being the root of the English word *"magic."*)

4. This review of evangelism relates to another form of the word that is a noun in English — evangelical. Modern usage has shifted the meaning of evangelical in an unbiblical way, bringing to mind fundamental/conservative, often non-mainstream denominations. However, the historic and best definition of **evangelical** is **"gospel-centered."** It may be difficult to reclaim this Biblical meaning, but it is nevertheless true.

5. **Doxology = speaking praise** is not in the Bible, but developed very early in the worship life of the Christian Church. It is made of two Greek words:

doxa - *ology*
(GLORY/PRAISE) (SPEAKING)

Sometimes used as a table prayer, a doxology is a joyful hymn of praise to God, usually as "Father, Son, and Holy Spirit/Ghost." There are three well-known forms:

"**Glory to God in the Highest ...**" (**Gloria in Excelsis**) used in worship and based on the angelic praise of Luke 2:14. The Christmas hymn "Angels We Have Heard on High" uses this Latin refrain fully spelled out: *Gloria in Excelsis Deo*, (**Glory in the Highest to God**);

"**Glory be to the Father and to the Son ...**" (**Gloria Patri**) also developed in worship, (**Glory to the Father**) and

"**Praise God From Whom All Blessings Flow**" — a well-known hymn from the 1600s.

6. Nor does it help to offer a definition simply from another language. Sacred and hallow(ed), for example, mean the same! Sacred = Latin for holy (*sacra*); Hallow(ed) = Old English for holy (*haalgian*).

7. The Hebrews have a word of similar meaning, **synagogue**. It is a Greek-based word meaning "assembly" or "meeting place," but was not used by Christians after they ceased worshiping in Jewish services by the end of the first century.

8. "**Catholic**" is the original word used in the Nicene Creed. The Reformation Period substituted "Christian" (from the German *Kristliche*) for **catholic** (from Latin *catholica* = **universal, encompassing**) in the Nicene Creed to distance themselves from what was seen as an erring institutional church. Recent definition as well as rekindled vision of the unity of all believers has prompted a return to the original "*catholica*" or catholic. The broad, expansive, and universal nature of the church is stressed, not any particular denomination.

9. Absent in the Revised Standard Version and New International Version, "communion" is translated only once by the New Revised Standard Version. It is in 2 Corinthians 13:13: "The grace of the Lord Jesus Christ, the love of God, and the communion (*koinonia*) of the Holy Spirit be with you all." (See Koinonia.)

10. The word "Holy" is used in front of God's Spirit because there are other kinds of (ungodly) "spirits." For example, there is a "spirit" or influence of the evil one (Ephesians 2:2). In addition, it is an enlightening use of words that alcohol is often called "spirits" because of its power to overcome its host. The tension is well put in Ephesians 5:18: "Do not get drunk with wine, for that is debauchery; but (instead) be filled with the Spirit."

11. The little word *el* (meaning God) often modifies others in the Old Testament, for example, where the word for "house" is *beth* — the city **Bethel** means "HOUSE OF GOD." **Emmanuel** (with us *is* God) is another example (also spelled **Immanuel**).

12. It is interesting how surprised many Christians are to realize the Fourth Commandment doesn't talk about *loving* father and mother. In a very helpful and practical way, it commands us to "honor" them. This is because Godly love cannot be felt in fullness in the human heart; nevertheless, we are at all times called to act (honor) in love.

13. From Old Testament days through modern observance by Orthodox Jews and "Seventh Day Adventists," the Sabbath is 24 hours of rest, and lasts from sundown Friday until sundown Saturday. This ancient practice explains why Jesus' proper burial by the women had to wait until daybreak on Sunday. Jesus died on "Good" Friday afternoon, and since it was nearly the Sabbath, which began at

sundown, Jesus' friends had to wait until the Sabbath was over (sundown Saturday) and for the next light (Sunday daybreak — Mark 16:1, 2) to complete burial preparations.

14. The opposite influence, of course, is God's Holy Spirit, who assumes the role of the defense counsel and brings into remembrance God's true word (John 14:26).

15. The opposite is true also. While satan is one who accuses God, the spirit and angels advocate his divine will. This is why the same Saint Paul who acknowledges his struggle with the evil one and the flesh can also refer to himself as an "angel" (Galatians 4:14)! The influence of each works in us all.

A Study Guide
Of Eight Sessions

1. Angels, Gospel, and Evangelism
   (To be, tell, and do the Good News)

2. Holy — Part 1
   (Holy, Holy Bible, Holy Thing = Sacrament, Holy Baptism, and Holy Communion)

3. Holy — Part 2
   (Holy Church, Saint, Holy Spirit)

4. Justification and Sanctification
   (God's accomplishments unfolding through us)

5. Disciple and Apostle
   (Learning to be Sent)

6. Lessons from Genesis
   (Adam, woman, naked, Eden, Nod, Genesis, and apple)

7. Love and Forgiveness
   (Kinds of love and practical forgiveness)

8. Making Numbers Count
   (The meaning of numbers in the Bible)

Session 1
Angels, Gospel, and Evangelism
To be, tell, and do the Good News

But the angel said to the women, "Do not be afraid; for I know that you seek Jesus who was crucified." (Matthew 28:5)

1. What is an angel? Discuss your personal beliefs as well as ideas and images throughout history. How are angels portrayed in the media?

2. What is the role of an angel in the Bible? **Read Angel, page 15.**

3. The primary purpose of an angel is to bring "news" from God — announcements of his will. **Read Gospel, page 28.** Gospel is literally "good news." Although angel and gospel are very different English words, they are forms of the same idea in the Biblical Greek:

> **Angels** — *aggelos*   (ANNOUNCEMENT/ers)
> bring *eu-aggelion* (GOOD-ANNOUNCEMENT)
>   **= Gospel**

Angels *are* what they say! So are Christians! How do you announce the Gospel? **Read 1 Corinthians 1:26—2:5** about how Paul did that. In what ways can you be an angel of God?

4. What Paul and Christians are to *do* with the gospel is "evangelism." Define evangelism. Where and how is it found in the Bible?

5. **Read Evangelism, page 25.** The English word "evangelism" is NOT in English Bibles! It is, nevertheless, a summary of many kinds of actions to "do" the Gospel. Evangelism is actually the

verb of Gospel. Think, for example, of a garden and of its care as gardening. That is how evangelism is to Gospel.

> **Angels** — *aggelos* (ANNOUNCEMENT/ers)
> bring ***eu**-aggelion* (GOOD-ANNOUNCEMENT)
> = **Gospel**
> by *eu-aggelizo* = **Gospeling!**

There is a wonderful and inspirational relationship unifying these three apparently different words. Whenever **angel, gospel,** and **evangelism** are used, think of the Gospel and your Christian calling to **be, tell,** and **do** the Good News.

In advertising, it is said "the medium is the message." How is this true of Christians?

Session 2
Holy — Part 1
Holy, Holy Bible, Holy Thing = Sacrament, Holy Baptism, and Holy Communion

For you are a people holy to the LORD your God, and the LORD has chosen you to be a people for his own possession, out of all the peoples that are on the face of the earth. (Deuteronomy 14:2)

1. Define the word "holy." List ways it is used in everyday speech.

2. Holy is an adjective, making its object "set apart" for God. **Read Holy, page 30.**

3. One of the most frequent uses of Holy is Holy Bible, often shortened to simply Bible. Discuss the word *Bible*. What is it? The word is not used in scripture, is it? Instead, God's written word is quoted by description, not title.
   For example,
   Read: Joshua 23:6 (law of Moses);
         Luke 24:44 (law, prophets, and psalms);
         2 Timothy 3:16, 17 (scripture).
   Read Holy Bible, page 31.

4. The Holy Bible is a means by which God's will is recalled and advanced. But it is static — it is written and is not rewritten. Therefore, there are other means by which God's will is conveyed. Discuss the word *Sacrament*. What is it? How many are there? Why are the sacraments described as "holy"? **Read Sacrament, page 46.**

5. Sacraments, as Bible, are **means by which God's will of setting apart his people is accomplished.**

> The Bible is a *record,*
> the sacraments are *actions.*

Holy means set apart for God's use. How do the Bible and Sacraments help God's people become holy?

Session 3
Holy — Part 2
Holy Church, Saint, Holy Spirit

Come to him, to that living stone, rejected by men but in God's sight chosen and precious; and like living stones be yourselves built into a spiritual house, to be a holy priesthood, to offer spiritual sacrifices acceptable to God through Jesus Christ. (1 Peter 2:4-5)

1. As review, use the verse above to define *holy*. How do phrases within the verse add meaning?

2. Discuss the word *church*. While Bible and Sacrament are not literally words in the Bible, church is. Read how church is used in
   1 Corinthians 1:2 (to the church);
   1 Corinthians 11:18 (as a church);
   1 Corinthians 16:19 (church in their house);
   Colossians 1:24 (Jesus' body).

3. What is the church? A place? A movement? A grouping? **Read Holy Church, page 31.**

4. The church is a *people* "called out" of sin and godlessness — an assembly of believers to exist and grow as the body of Christ. In what ways does the church show herself to be the Body of Christ? What are the church's shortcomings?

5. The Holy Church (assembly) (set aside for God's use) is made up of Holy Ones (saints) (set aside for God's use).
   But what is a saint? Someone living? Dead? An extraordinary person? Explain whether or not you are a saint! Then read
   Romans 1:7 (called to be saints);

Romans 12:12-13 (living faithful);
Colossians 1:2; Ephesians 4:12 (faithful departed);
1 Thessalonians 3:11-13 (departed returning with Jesus).

Read Saint, page 46.

6. All Christians living and departed are saints (ones) (set apart for God) by virtue of God's calling out to be the body of Christ, the Church (assembly of believers) (set apart for God). Christians are bound ("sealed" in Holy Baptism liturgy) into one unit by means of the Holy Spirit. As background to the role of the Spirit, read from the following samples of Scripture:
Genesis 1:1-3 (creating force)
Genesis 6:3 (human life force)
John 14:26 (teacher)
John 20:22, 23 (authority to forgive)
Acts 1:8 (empowerment to witness)
1 Corinthians 6:19 (resident within)
1 Corinthians 12:3 (sustains faith)
Hebrews 2:4 (bestows gifts — see also 1 Corinthians 12—14)
2 Peter 1:20-21 (authority behind God's word)

How do you experience the presence and power of the Holy Spirit?

7. Much more than a *place*, the Holy Church is a *movement* of Holy People (Saints), unified by the *power*, the Holy Spirit.
As a concluding study, recall hymns about the Holy Spirit and how you and the church of God are influenced.

Session 4
Justification and Sanctification
God's accomplishments unfolding through us

And we all, with unveiled face, beholding the glory of the Lord, are being changed into his likeness from one degree of glory to another; for this comes from the Lord who is the Spirit. (2 Corinthians 3:18)

1. Why is so much emphasis placed on two seemingly difficult words as justification and sanctification? What meaning do you place on each?

2. The subtitle above gives a clue to the unique and powerful meanings of these two words.
    Justification relates to God's *accomplishments, things done.*
    Sanctification relates to the *process* of God's accomplishments *unfolding.*
    The difference is the key to understanding much of Christian theology and life. Recall the word *saint*, for example **(page 46)**. Are you a saint? (Yes, by God's redemption and declaration in Jesus — *justification.*) Are you saintly in all your actions? (No, that is the ongoing process of becoming what God has declared us to be — *sanctification.*) Discuss how this distinction between saint and saintly shows itself in your life.

3. *Justification* is a word that has a different meaning today than in biblical times. Consider, for example, the American justice system. The foundation is "innocent until proven guilty." People today expect God to think that way also, don't they? Consider the idea, for example, "Well, I'm not *so bad*, surely God will accept me." But how does this view compare with these passages?
    Read Psalm 53:2-3 (none do good) and
    Romans 3:19-20 (there is nothing we can do).

4. **Read Justification, page 36.** Justification in the Bible and in Lutheran theology is just the opposite of the modern definition. Justification is the execution of a deserved penalty, accomplished once and for all by Jesus Christ. How does that make you feel? What can you do in response?

5. Christian response is the key behind **sanctification.** It is a process. While declared perfect (sins white as snow and forgotten by God — justification), Christians will only struggle to live out a perfect life. Read of Paul's awareness (and frustration) in **Romans 7:15—8:6.**

6. Is there any doubt Paul was both saved and a saint? We, too, are both while still contending with the consequences of sin. That "contention" is the realm of sanctification — becoming *sanctus*, that is, holy = set apart for God. It is a lifelong process for those who have received salvation.

7. If you were asked, "Will you go to heaven when you die?" what would you answer? Is there any biblical reason for a Christian not being certain of salvation?

8. Read a comparison of justification and sanctification in the article on **1 = unity, page 9.** Christians are certain of salvation because it is God's doing, received by faith — the power and authority are his. We may feel anguish in our inability to live up to our calling, but that, too, is forgiven while remaining a goal.

9. What specific goals toward becoming holy do you currently have? (Sanctification process)

How does God's grace = undeserved love assist you? (Justification reality)

Session 5
Disciple and Apostle
Learning to be Sent

Then he said to his disciples, "The harvest is plentiful, but the laborers are few; pray therefore the Lord of the harvest to send out laborers into his harvest." And he called to him his twelve disciples and gave them authority over unclean spirits, to cast them out, and to heal every disease and every infirmity. (Matthew 9:37—10:1)

1. **Read Matthew 5:1-12.** What are the roles of the disciples of Jesus? In what ways are we disciples of Jesus?

2. Disciples are to learn. But when is graduation? Is there a point where the student becomes greater than the teacher? It happens in classrooms all the time, doesn't it? The answer relates to that distinction between justification and sanctification — while declared perfect, we can only strive to live up to that declaration. Jesus, who saves perfectly, noted in Luke 6:40-42 that, although a disciple may be like the teacher, the disciple will not surpass the teacher (however, you never surpass Jesus). Compare this to the end time revelation in 1 John 3:2 (when we will be as he is).

3. A disciple is a student, albeit in a continuous growth process. But how great are the demands expected of us? On the one hand, they seem conclusive, almost easy: **Read Matthew 10:42** (give a cup of water). On the other hand, they seem impossible to achieve: **Read Luke 14:26-33** (renounce all — although the issue is priorities, not a negation of the Fourth Commandment). The key to meaningful discipleship is summed up well in Jesus' famous words of ethic — **read Luke 10:25-37** (love the Lord; the Good Samaritan). The expectation is both obvious and absolute — respond to anyone to whom you are a neighbor and let nothing be more important than representing Jesus.

4. Did you notice how being a **disciple = learner** cannot help but become an **apostle = one who is sent**? It is clear the biblical word *apostle* referred to the twelve, or the inner circle, of disciples. But is there any reason Christians today cannot be thought of as apostles = ones sent? No! Once a person comes to faith and realizes the need to learn and grow into the image of Jesus, what is the next expected consequence? Evangelism! Review how evangelism is the verb — the doing — of the gospel. **See Evangelism, page 25.**

5. Saint Paul had a useful idea for disciples striving to be apostles. His method was simple: "Be imitators of me, as I am of Christ" (1 Corinthians 11:1). Imitation was his suggestion, and isn't this in line with the end of the Good Samaritan parable ("Go, and do likewise")?

6. In what way are you both a disciple of Jesus (a learner) as well as a modern-day apostle of Jesus (one sent)? What can you do to grow in each area?

Session 6
Lessons from Genesis
Adam, woman, naked, Eden, Nod, Genesis, and apple

Then Cain went away from the presence of the LORD, and dwelt in the land of Nod, east of Eden. (Genesis 4:16)

What do the seven words above have in common? They all relate to the beginning chapters of the Bible (**see Genesis = beginning, page 27**). The first eleven chapters of Genesis uniquely contain many plays on words or hidden (in English) meanings to teach a lesson. Here is a brief summary that will help in appreciating these instructive "beginnings."

1. What is the meaning of your name? The name Adam is one of the first name-lessons in the Bible. There are many instances where God changed or gave a name in order to teach a lesson. **See Isaac, page 34**, for example. Just as many names today have traditional meanings, even more so ancient names carried meanings. **Read Adam, page 13**.

2. *Adam* means "ground," and is to teach that we are "but dust, and to dust we shall return" (from Ash Wednesday liturgy). Incidentally, *Eve* has a unique meaning also — it is defined in Genesis 3:20.

3. Once man's relationship to the earth and God's spirit is given (Genesis 2:7), other relationships develop, beginning between man and God, then man and others. Eden was the perfect realm God had originally made for us. That idyllic realm was forever shattered by the fall into sin. **Read Genesis 2:21—3:21**.

4. There are some extraordinary universal lessons in this section. Can you list some?

5. Some of those lessons relate to the words:
   - **naked**. Adam and Eve had nothing of which to be ashamed in the beginning. But that changed after the fall into sin. **Read Naked, page 41**. This imagery is little used in the Bible, but it is rich in symbolism. Despite God's disappointment and anger with Adam and Eve, "the LORD God made for Adam and for his wife garments of skins, and clothed them" (Genesis 3:21). This is the first act of grace God displayed in response to sin. Paul continued this imagery in Galatians 3:27.
   - **Eden and Nod**. The saga of falling into sin continued with the offspring of Adam and Eve. Cain and Abel contested for God's favor and Abel was slain. As a consequence, Cain not only was denied Eden, but also he was expelled into Nod. **Read Eden, page 23**. Again, Paul used this imagery in 2 Timothy 4:3-5.
   - **apple**. What was the fruit Adam and Eve shared? **Read Apple, page 16**. In fine biblical tradition, *apple* is an example of words that teach a lesson.

6. In conclusion, share the gospel using the *ideas* of Genesis 2 and 3, comparing Adam and Eve in Eden with the apple and sin and God's response, with men and women in the world of temptation and of God's response.

Session 7
Love and Forgiveness
Kinds of love and practical forgiveness

And walk in love, as Christ loved us and gave himself up for us, a fragrant offering and sacrifice to God. (Ephesians 5:2)

1. Is there more than one kind of love? Between siblings, sexes, mates, citizens, and believers? How are they different?

2. **Read John 21:15-17.** Why do you think Jesus asked Peter the same question so many times?

3. **Read and discuss Love, page 38.**

4. Is love for you an emotion or an action or both? What is Christ's love? What is Christian love?

5. Love again relates to justification and sanctification — it is accomplished and also at the same time unfolding. That tension shows itself in a primary manifestation of love — forgiveness. If we are to love as Christ has loved us, then why are criminals not forgiven and freed or loved ones released from ill will?

6. **Read about Forgiveness, page 26.**

7. In which ways can you forgive someone without forgetting a wrong? Considering parents, siblings, spouse, or neighbors, conclude this session by explaining how love can be

   A) an action without necessarily an emotion,
   B) an absolution without necessarily a concession.

Session 8
Making Numbers Count
The meaning of numbers in the Bible

Then Peter came up and said to him, "Lord, how often shall my brother sin against me, and I forgive him? As many as seven times?" Jesus said to him, "I do not say to you seven times, but seventy times seven." (Matthew 18:21-22)

1. Numbers themselves may seem dry or irrelevant, but that is because numbers no longer carry the symbolism they had in ages past. Or do they? What does 13 mean? How many hotels have a thirteenth floor on the elevator? Is "zillion" a real number?

2. There are two groupings to help appreciate biblical numbers — one grouping is the basic building blocks of 1, 3, 4, and 10. The other grouping is combinations of those building blocks, such as 7, 12, and squares of 10. These fundamentals help interpret the 70 x 7 in the text above, or the controversial number of 144,000 in Revelation.

3. Review the first group of the building blocks by reading
   1, page 9
   3, page 10
   4, page 10 and
   10, page 11.

Before proceeding, what do you think these combinations might suggest:

        3 (God) + 4 (world) = ?
        3 x 4 = ?
        4 x 10 = ?

4. Review basic combinations of
   7, page 10 and
   12, page 11.

5. With these foundations in mind, what is the meaning of forgiveness being commanded **70 x 7**? Read the verses at the heading, then see **page 12**.

6. Is **144,000** of Revelation 14:1, 3 (read it) a literal or symbolic number? Discuss, then **see page 12**.

7. Think about your sanctuary — what biblical numbers are found in artwork, architecture, or symbols, and what meaning do they convey? Keeping these basic numerical expressions in mind can help interpret and highlight God's word. For after all, God uses everything he can to express his will, even making sure "numbers count"![1]

---

1. One must be careful, however, not to overdo these things. A number may simply be that. It is useful to look for deeper meanings — just be aware they are not always there! In addition, some numbers have very questionable meanings. A classic example is **666** of Revelation 13:18. The best studies suggest it is the symbolic addition of the letters of a person's name. In this case, 666 (as well as an alternate 616) are the **"value" of ancient letters** in the names Nero as well as Caligula (both of whom were feared Roman Emperors and terrible persecutors of the Church).

Index

1	9	Church	19, 31
3	10	Church Year	19
4	10	City of David	53
7	10	Clergy	37
10	11	Communion	33
12	11	Concord	20
40	12	Covenant	48
144,000	12	Creed	20
70 x 7	12	David	35
Abba	13	Devil	20
Abraham	13	Disciple	21
Abram	13	Doxology	54
Adam	13	Easter	20, 22
Adonai	52	Ecclesiastical	32
Advent	14, 20	Ecumenical	23
Agape	14, 39	Eden	23
Alleluia	14	Epiphany	20, 24
Alpha	15	Epistle	24
Amen	15	Emmanuel	55
Angel	15	Eucharist	24
Apostle	16, 21	Evangelical	54
Apple	16	Evangelism	25
Ascension	16, 20	Eve	14
Atonement	16	Evil	16, 26
Baptism	17	Expiation	36
Benediction	17	Forgiveness	26, 50
Bethel	55	Genesis	27, 53
Bible	18, 31	Gentile	54
Book of Concord	20	Gloria in Excelsis	54
Brood of vipers	41	Gloria Patri	54
Catechism	18	Glory	27
Catholic	55	God	51
Charismatic	18	Good News	28
Christ	19	Gospel	28
Christian	19	Grace	18, 29

Halleluia	29	Prophecy	45
Halloween	29	Prophesy	45
Holy	30	Rabbi	21
Holy Bible	31	Repent	45
Holy Church	31	Sabbath	45, 55
Holy Communion	33	Sacrament	46
Holy Spirit	33	Saint	46
Hosanna	34	Salutation	47
Immanuel	55	Sanctification	10, 39, 47
Isaac	34	Satan	48
Israel	35	Shalom	49
Jehovah	52	Sin	49
Jerusalem	35, 53	Spirit	33, 50, 55
Jesus	35	Sunday	50
Justification	10, 36, 39	Synagogue	55
Kirche	31	Testament	48
Koinonia	36	Theology	51
Kyrie	37	Translation	51
Laity	37	Trinity	51
Lectionary	19	Woman	14
Lent	20, 38	Yahweh	51
Liturgy	38	YHWH	35, 52
LORD	52	Yom Kippur	17
Lord's Supper	24	Zion	53
Love	38		
Magi	54		
Man	14		
Messiah	41		
Naked	41		
Nave	42		
Nod	23, 42		
Omega	15		
Paraclete	43		
Paschal	43		
Passover	43		
Pentecost	20, 44		
Peter	44